SHORT WALKS NORTHUMBERLAND

WOOLER, ROTHBURY, ALNWICK AND THE COAST

by Vivienne Crow

CICERONE

Northumberland has many miles of beautiful coast path (Walk 13)

CONTENTS

USING THIS GUIDE

Routes in this book

In this book you will find a selection of easy or moderate walks suitable for almost everyone, including casual walkers and families with children, or for when you only have a short time to fill. The routes have been carefully chosen to allow you to explore the area and its attractions. Most routes are circular or out-and-back, although some linear walks may be included that use public transport to get back to the start. Although there may be some climbs there is no challenging terrain, but do bear in mind that conditions can sometimes be wet or muddy underfoot. A route summary table is included on page 6 to help you choose the right walk.

Clothing and footwear

You won't need any special equipment to enjoy these walks. The weather in Britain can be changeable, so choose clothing suitable for the season and wear or carry a waterproof jacket. For footwear, comfortable walking boots or trainers with a good grip are best. A small rucksack for drinks, snacks and spare clothing is useful. See www.adventuresmart.uk.

Walk descriptions

At the beginning of each walk you'll find all the information you need:

- start/finish location, with postcode and a what3words address to help you find it

- parking and transport information, estimated walking time, total distance and climb

- details of public toilets available along the route and where you can get refreshments

- a summary of the key highlights of the walk and what you might see

Timings given are the time to complete the walk at a reasonable walking pace. Allow extra time for extended stops or if walking with children.

The route is described in clear, easy-to-follow directions, with each waypoint marked on an accompanying map extract. It's a good idea to read the whole of the route instructions before setting out, so that you know what to expect.

Maps, GPX files and what3words

Extracts from the OS® 1:25,000 map accompany each route. GPX files for all the walks in this book are available to download at www.cicerone.co.uk/1201/gpx.

What3words is a free smartphone app which identifies every 3m square of the globe with a unique three-word address, e.g. ///destiny.cafe.sonic. For more information see https://what3words.com/products/what3words-app.

Walking with children

Even young children can be surprisingly strong walkers, but every family is different and you may need to adapt the timings given in this book to take that into account. Make sure you go at the pace of the slowest member and choose a walk with an exciting objective in mind, such as a cave, river, waterfall or picnic spot. Many of the walks can be shortened to suit – suggestions are included at the end of the route description.

Dogs

Sheep or cattle may be found grazing on a number of these walks. Keep dogs under control at all times so that they don't scare or disturb livestock or wildlife. Cattle, particularly cows with calves, may very occasionally pose a risk to walkers with dogs. If you ever feel threatened by cattle, you should let go of your dog's lead and let it run free.

Enjoying the countryside responsibly

Enjoy the countryside and treat it with respect to protect our natural environments. Stick to footpaths and take your litter home with you. When driving, slow down on rural roads and park considerately, or better still use public transport. For more details check out www.gov.uk/countryside-code.

The Countryside Code

Respect everyone
- be considerate to those living in, working in and enjoying the countryside
- leave gates and property as you find them
- do not block access to gateways or driveways when parking
- be nice, say hello, share the space
- follow local signs and keep to marked paths unless wider access is available

Protect the environment
- take your litter home – leave no trace of your visit
- do not light fires and only have BBQs where signs say you can
- always keep dogs under control and in sight
- dog poo – bag it and bin it – any public waste bin will do
- care for nature – do not cause damage or disturbance

Enjoy the outdoors
- check your route and local conditions
- plan your adventure – know what to expect and what you can do
- enjoy your visit, have fun, make a memory

ROUTE SUMMARY TABLE

WALK NAME	START POINT	TIME	DISTANCE
1. St Mary's Island	Near Hartley	1¼hr	3.5km (2¼ miles)
2. Northumberlandia	Near Cramlington	1¼hr	3km (1¾ miles)
3. Simonside Hills	Rothbury	4¼hr	13.5km (8½ miles)
4. Rothbury Terraces	Rothbury	2hr	6km (3¾ miles)
5. South from Amble	Amble	2¼hr	7.5km (4¾ miles)
6. North from Alnmouth	Alnmouth	1¾hr	5km (3 miles)
7. Alnwick Castle and riverside	Alnwick	1¼hr	4km (2½ miles)
8. Brough Law	Ingram	2hr	6km (3¾ miles)
9. Craster and Dunstanburgh Castle	Craster	1¾hr	5.5km (3½ miles)
10. Newton-by-the-Sea	High Newton	2¼hr	7.5km (4¾ miles)
11. St Cuthbert's Way from Wooler	Wooler	2¾hr	8.5km (5¼ miles)
12. Wooler Common	Wooler	2½hr	6.5km (4 miles)
13. Bamburgh	Bamburgh	2hr	7km (4¼ miles)
14. Holy Island (Lindisfarne)	Holy Island	1¾hr	6km (3¾ miles)
15. Berwick-upon-Tweed	Berwick-upon-Tweed	1½hr	5km (3 miles)

HIGHLIGHTS

Tidal island, lighthouse and grey seals

Human landform sculpture

Ridgewalk, sandstone formations and prehistoric rock 'art'

Heather moorland and amazing views

Sand dunes, quiet hamlets and wildlife

Low cliffs, pretty river, estuary, beachside path

Lovely old town and riverside meadows with castle views

Low hills, prehistoric features and views

Fishing village, coast and castle ruins

Pretty village, dunes, beaches and nature reserve

Moorland, wildlife and views

Edge of the Cheviot Hills, woods and views

Coast, castle and historic village

Tidal island, dunes, castle and priory ruins

Historic town walls and riverside path

SYMBOLS USED ON ROUTE MAPS

(S) Start point

(F) Finish point

(SF) Start and finish at the same place

[4] → Waypoint

〜 Route line

MAPPING IS SHOWN AT A SCALE OF 1:25,000

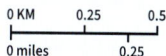

```
0 KM        0.25        0.5
|-----------|-----------|
0 miles              0.25
```

DOWNLOAD THE GPX FILES FOR FREE AT
www.cicerone.co.uk/1201/gpx

East Hill seen from the initial climb from Ingram (Walk 8)

INTRODUCTION

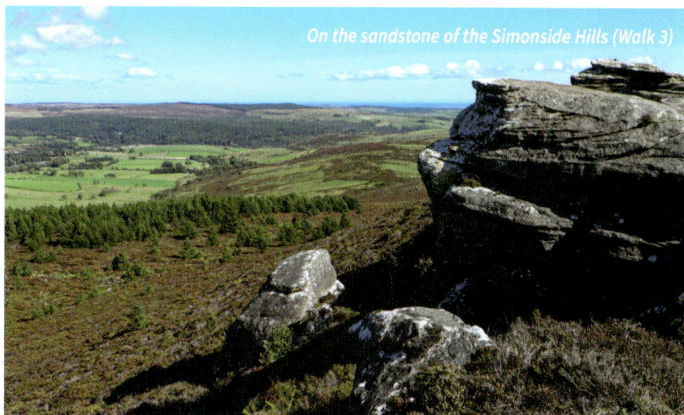
On the sandstone of the Simonside Hills (Walk 3)

For anyone who loves the countryside, Northumberland has lots to offer, from seemingly endless beaches to rolling hills and sprawling forests. For those who want to see wildlife, there's everything here from seals to the waders who return to the uplands every spring. If it's history you're after, the artefacts scattered throughout the county cover a massive time span – from prehistoric 'rock art' and medieval castles to the coastal defences built in World War 2.

Throw in an intricate network of paths and trails, as well as significant areas of access land, and you've got a region that is perfect for anyone wanting to explore on foot one of England's least densely populated counties.

Increasingly, people come to Northumberland to escape the frenetic pace of urban life; to absorb the peace and tranquillity of its wide, open spaces and to gaze up at its big, big skies. The welcome you'll receive here is legendary too; whether you're a day visitor looking for an after-walk cafe or a holiday-maker in search of a friendly B&B.

What to expect

This book covers a long, narrow strip of land down the eastern side of Northumberland, from its North Sea coast to the edge of the Northumberland National Park. The walks, all of which are circular, stretch from St Mary's Island in the south – just within Tyne and Wear – up to Berwick-upon-Tweed, England's most northerly town. The distance between these two, by road, is about 100km, while the distance between the coast and the westernmost routes at Rothbury is less than 35km.

The walks are designed to cater for most abilities. They can be completed at any time of the year, although you may encounter ice or snow in the winter. It's also worth remembering that, although Northumberland is on the eastern side of the country and is therefore drier than many parts of northern England, it can get extremely cold when an easterly wind blows in off the North Sea in the winter.

More than half of the 15 walks include sections of the coast, many within the Northumberland Coast National Landscape. These tend to be the easiest walks in the book. The scenery here includes vast dune systems, long beaches and picturesque fishing villages such as Craster and Low Newton-by-the-Sea. Two tidal islands are visited – Holy Island (or Lindisfarne) and the tiny St Mary's Island – as well as some of the UK's most impressively located castles. These include Bamburgh, Lindisfarne and the romantic, cliff-perched ruins of Dunstanburgh Castle.

Inland, the walks cover the unique human landform sculpture of Northumberlandia and the historic town of Alnwick, as well as the low hills and heather moorland along the eastern edge of the National Park. The latter includes a 'challenge route' (Walk 3) that climbs onto the Simonside Hills, a windswept ridge of sculpted sandstone outcrops that enjoys far-reaching views in all directions.

Where to stay

If you're planning to explore eastern Northumberland, there are a number of places that make a good base. For the southern half of the region, Rothbury and Alnwick have a decent range of accommodation – including hostels, B&Bs, hotels and self-catering cottages – as well as a variety of shops, cafes and pubs. Alnwick also has a number of other visitor attractions, including its castle and the Alnwick Garden.

Further north, Wooler offers a warm welcome with a similar range of facilities to Rothbury and Alnwick plus large campsites. On rainy days, the Ad Gefrin whisky distillery and Anglo-Saxon museum is well worth a visit.

Those in tents, motorhomes or caravans will find numerous campsites dotted along the coast, although many of these do get booked up early for the main school holidays.

Bamburgh Castle (Walk 13)

Berwick-upon-Tweed, Bamburgh, Craster, Alnmouth and Amble are also geared up for holidaymakers.

Travel

The eastern side of Northumberland is served by the East Coast Main Line railway. After calling at Newcastle upon Tyne on their way from London to Edinburgh, trains stop at Morpeth, Alnmouth and Berwick-upon-Tweed.

Some of the key buses for anyone planning to use public transport to walk the routes in this book include the X18 from Newcastle to Berwick-upon-Tweed, which runs roughly every hour and calls in at Amble, Alnmouth, Alnwick, Craster and Bamburgh among other towns and villages along the coast. Another hourly service, the X20 runs between Newcastle and Alnwick,

calling in at Amble and Alnmouth, while the 418 connects Alnwick with Belford via Craster, High Newton-by-the-Sea and Bamburgh.

Wooler and Rothbury are served by a number of local buses, and even Holy Island is on the route of a regular bus – the 477 from Berwick. Only Ingram stands out as being without a regular service.

If you're planning to use public transport, the best resource is the Traveline – www.traveline.info.

For those travelling to Holy Island via private transport, it is important to remember that the island is linked to the mainland by a causeway that disappears twice a day when it is inundated by the incoming tide. Check the safe times for crossing at https://holyislandcrossingtimes.northumberland.gov.uk.

WALK 1
St Mary's Island

Time 1¼hr
Distance 3.5km
(2¼ miles)
Climb 20m

Easy walking across a causeway to reach a lighthouse on a tiny, tidal island

Start/finish	*Old Hartley road-end*
Locate	*NE26 4RB ///paid.lined.dared*
Cafes/pubs	*None on route*
Transport	*Bus 308 stops within 10min walk of start point*
Parking	*Free car park at Old Hartley road-end*
Toilets	*Public toilets in St Mary's Island north car park*

Easy-going paths lead to and from the causeway to St Mary's Island – a delightful place where grey seals haul out and visitors come to climb to the top of the lighthouse. Check tide times before setting out because the causeway is only open for a few hours either side of low tide. Lighthouse opening and safe crossing times can be found at my.northtyneside. gov.uk.

Blue skies over the coast near St Mary's Island

13

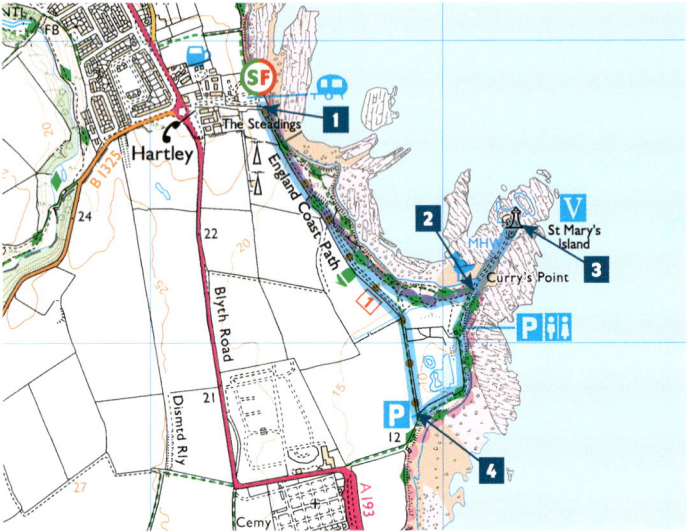

On the causeway to the island

1 Follow the broad, surfaced path from the road-end car park, so that you have the sea on your left. Having followed this path for 470m, fork left at an England Coast Path waymark. Keep left at the next fork, staying with the clearest path, later passing a row of benches and descending some steps.

2 At the bottom of the steps, turn left to cross the causeway. Follow the surfaced lane right up to the cottages on **St Mary's Island** and then climb the steps on the right to reach the lighthouse. Visitors are welcome to complete a circuit of the built area, but people are requested to keep off the rocks to protect the wildlife.

3 Leaving the island, recross the causeway and follow the road past the first car park – the 'north' car park – which has public toilets in it. A trail to the right of the road then continues to a second car park – the 'south' car park.

4 From the far end of this second car park, take the surfaced path on the right. This passes to the left of the tiny St Mary's Island Wetland Reserve. Beyond the reserve, keep left as a lesser trail goes right, later rejoining your outward route to return to the car park where the walk started.

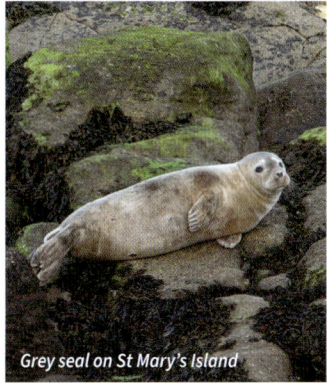
Grey seal on St Mary's Island

Grey seals, basking on the rocks, can be observed from the walled area surrounding the lighthouse complex. Females are grey with black spots, while males are generally darker with grey spots.

▬ To shorten

Park at St Mary's Island 'north' car park and join the walk at Waypoint 2 to cross the causeway and then return to the same car park. This cuts the walk by about 45min.

St Mary's Lighthouse

The current lighthouse on St Mary's Island was built in 1898, although monks maintained a lantern to warn passing ships of the rocks from as early as the 11th century. The lighthouse was decommissioned in 1984 and was opened as a visitor attraction soon after. Today, visitors can climb the 137 steps to the lantern room at the top of the lighthouse. Exhibits on the ground floor explain the lighthouse's history and provide information about the local wildlife, including the wildflowers, waders and various seabirds that can be seen on the wetland reserve on the mainland.

The site has good, surfaced paths

WALK 2
Northumberlandia

Time 1¼hr
Distance 3km
(1¾ miles)
Climb 45m

A unique and fascinating stroll onto a human landform sculpture

Start/finish	Northumberlandia, near Cramlington
Locate	NE23 8AU ///hospitals.copiers.thudding
Cafes/pubs	Cafe on site
Transport	Buses X22 and X21 stop within 10min walk of site
Parking	Northumberlandia car park, Blagdon Lane
Toilets	At visitor centre/cafe

You're unlikely to forget Northumberlandia in a hurry. Known as the Lady of the North, it's a sculpture of a reclining woman, created by shaping piles of rock and soil. Featuring wildflower-rich grassland and ponds that are home to waterfowl and dragonflies, the site is managed by Northumberland Wildlife Trust. Visitors can follow paths around the artwork and up to a high point of 30m on its face.

The cafe at Northumberlandia

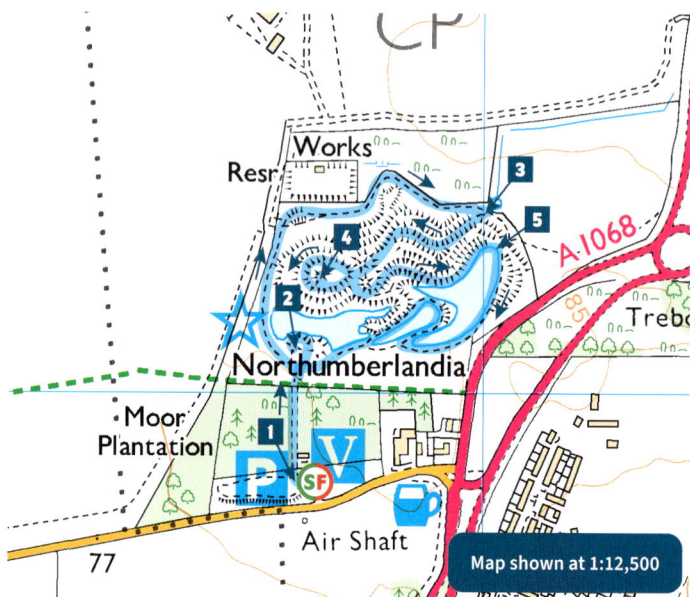

Map shown at 1:12,500

1 From the car park, walk to the site entrance and follow the path straight ahead beside the **visitor centre/cafe**. Emerging from the trees, you reach a crossing of ways. Take the middle of three options ahead and then fork left. The trail corkscrews its way onto a stone-crowned mound providing a view of this part of the site.

2 From the top of the mound, return to the crossing of routes and turn right. This surfaced path skirts the outside edge of the landform. In early summer, the grassland at the base of the sculpture is full of colour, thanks to the wildflowers allowed to proliferate here. After the path swings right, pass one gravel path to the right, followed by a grass path. Soon after a bench, you'll see two paths close together on the right.

3 Take the second of these two paths, climbing steadily onto the sculpture's 'body'. Keep left at an early fork. After joining a path from the right, turn right along a gravel path. At the top of the next slight rise, where the path splits again, keep straight ahead. You quickly reach a path junction on the lady's 'neck'. Take the

Exploring Northumberlandia

second path from the right, climbing on the 'head'. Climb the first set of steps on the left and then keep left to follow the path uphill to the 'face', the highest point on the sculpture. From here, as well as getting a bird's eye view of the artwork, you look out across the surrounding countryside.

4 From the top, follow the path back down the steps and bear left to complete a circuit of the head. Returning to the 'neck' path junction, turn right. Take the next broad, grass path on the left – 70m beyond the 'neck'. This drops to a large pond,

fringed by bullrushes. Walk with the water on your right to reach the gravel perimeter path.

> **A memorial stone near this junction remembers Cramlington Airfield, built nearby in 1915 in response to German Zeppelin airship raids over Tyneside. Three fighters of the Royal Flying Corps, later the Royal Air Force, were based here. The airfield was abandoned in the 1930s.**

5 Turn right along the gravel, still with the pond on your right. At the next gravel

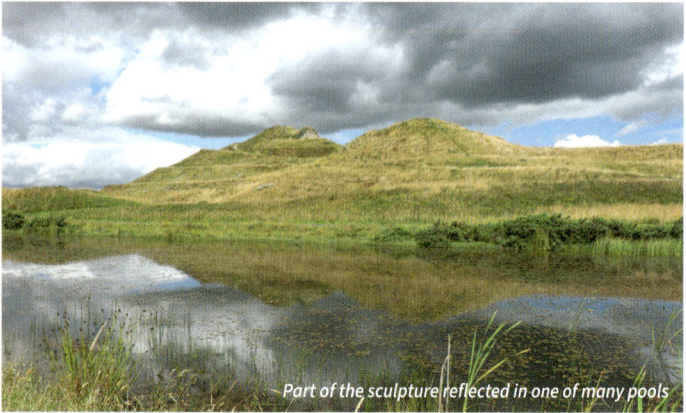

Part of the sculpture reflected in one of many pools

junction, turn right again, to walk around another, smaller pond. Keep right on rejoining the perimeter path, and soon return to the junction where your circuit of the site began. Turn left to retrace your steps to the cafe and car park.

✚ To lengthen

Having completed the walk, spend 10 or 15min exploring the small area of woodland between the sculpture and the car park.

Human landform sculpture

Construction on Northumberlandia started in 2010. The £3m project was part of a partnership between the landowner, the Blagdon Estate, and the Banks Group, which runs the adjacent Shotton surface coal mine. The aim was to create a new landscape for the community to enjoy while mining continues. The sculpture itself was the work of the US-born landscape architect Charles Jencks, who spent much of the last two decades of his life designing landforms and symbolic landscapes.

WALK 3
Simonside Hills

CHALLENGE ROUTE

Time 4¼hr
Distance 13.5km (8½ miles)
Climb 470m

A long route including forest, prehistoric features and an amazing ridge walk

Start/finish	*Market Cross, Rothbury*
Locate	*NE65 7UT ///dusts.flotation.minus*
Cafes/pubs	*In Rothbury*
Transport	*Buses 16A, 16B, 471 and X14 serve Rothbury*
Parking	*Cowhaugh car park (free) beside River Coquet, Rothbury*
Toilets	*Rothbury town centre*

After a steady climb from Rothbury, first beside the River Coquet and then through forests, you reach the base of Simonside. A short but steep pull leads onto the ridge, studded with sandstone formations sculpted by the elements. Far-reaching views are enjoyed as you stride out along the constructed path along this windswept line of high ground. The gentle descent back to the town passes close to an Iron Age fort and prehistoric 'rock art'.

The River Coquet

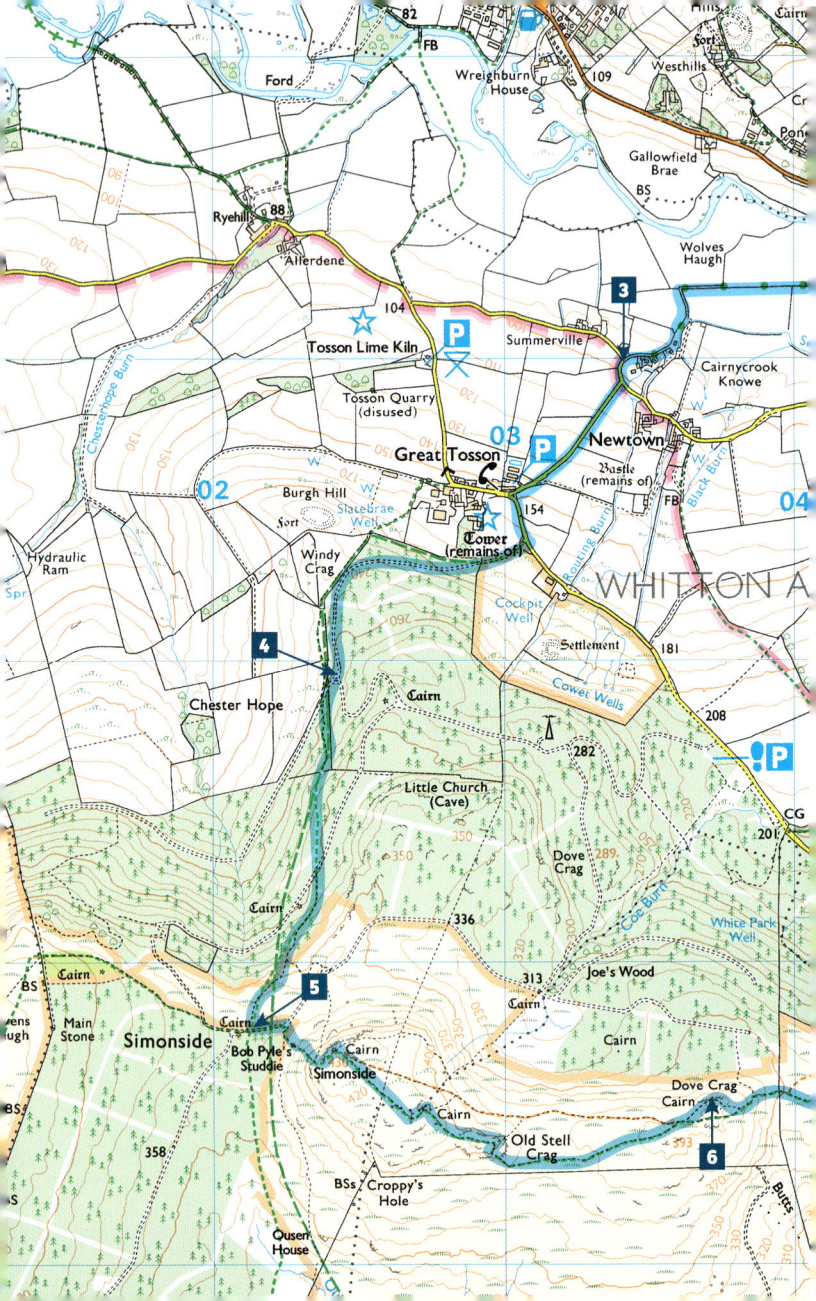

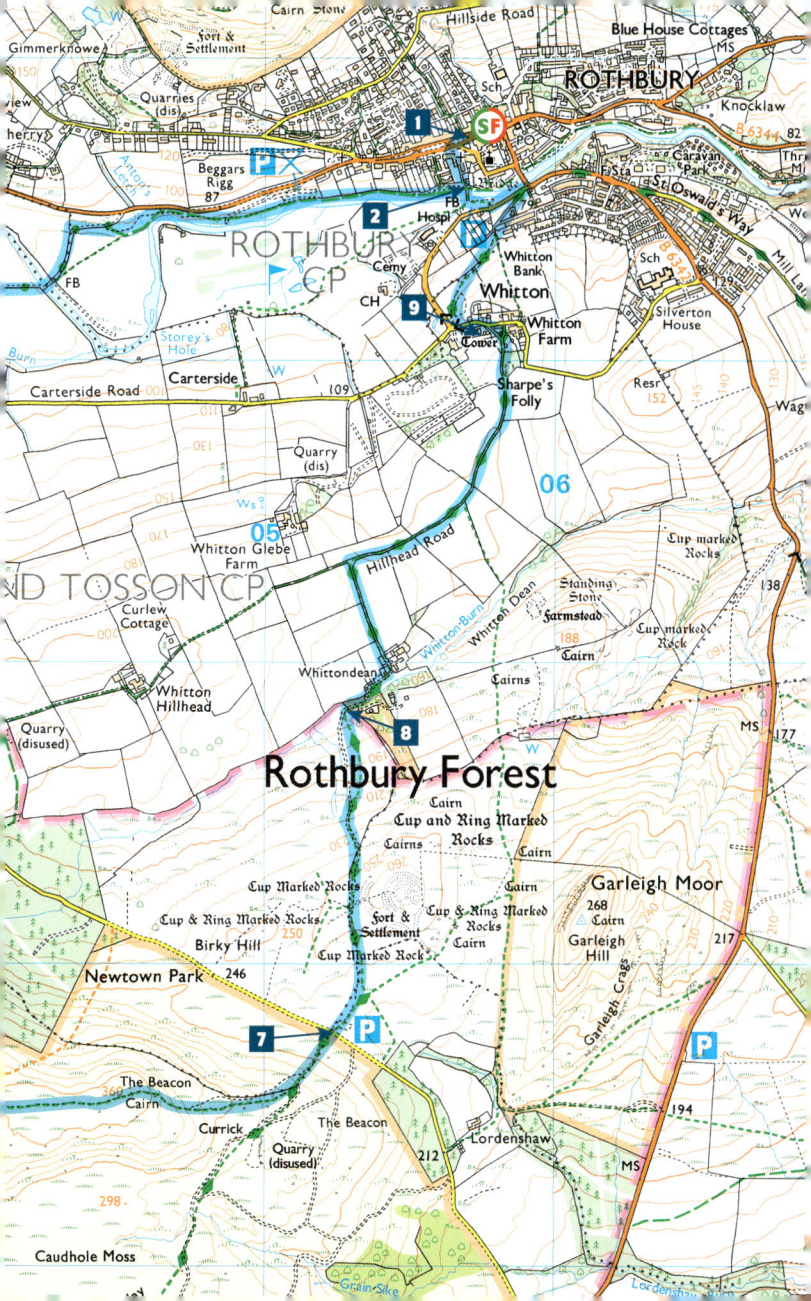

Enjoying the views from the Simonside Hills

1 Standing on Front Street with your back to the Market Cross, turn left. Immediately after crossing the junction with Church Street, go left again and then keep straight ahead along the passageway to the right of the United Reformed Church. Continue straight on to reach the **River Coquet**. If you've parked at the riverside car park cross a footbridge to join the walk here.

2 Turn right along the riverside path. This ends at a gate, about 1.5km into the walk. Go through and turn left to drop to a **footbridge**. Cross and walk the field edge with a fence on your left. This path later becomes a farm track. Follow the track to the left. Join a surfaced lane near some cottages and follow it to a minor road.

3 Turn left at this T-junction and take the next road on the right. Go left at the road junction in **Great Tosson** and, in 150m, go through a gate set back on the right.

The ruined tower near the junction in Great Tosson is the remains of a pele tower, built about 600 years ago by the Ogles, a powerful local family. This fortified home acted as a stronghold against both Scottish raiders and marauding Border Reivers.

A path leads up to the forest, entered via another gate. A track now rises steadily through the trees. Continue along it for 800m to reach a fork.

4 Bear right at this fork, briefly heading downhill. In another 100m, bear left along a narrower trail through the trees and bracken. After 600m, this emerges on a broader path in a clearing. Turn right and immediately go left along a trail with a red waymark beside it. At a fork where the red Forestry England route goes left, keep straight on, soon reaching a broad track.

5 Turn left along the track. When it bends left, turn right and take the clear path climbing left. A short, steep climb leads to **Simonside**, crowned by a cairn and with views of the distant North Sea. Follow the flagstone path along the crest of the high ground. It passes another sandstone outcrop and cairn and then descends through **Old Stell Crag**. The next top is **Dove Crag**, topped by a burial cairn.

6 Descend from Dove Crag. As the red waymarked route goes left, keep right. Follow the pitched path down to a gate and then continue to the final top on the ridge – **The Beacon** – also topped by an ancient cairn. As you descend, the Lordenshaw hill fort is visible to the northeast. Bear left at a way-marked junction to drop to the road

Views back towards the Cheviot Hills

7 Cross over and walk to the far side of the **Lordenshaw car park** to pick up a path through the grass. There are lots of trails in this area, so be careful to keep to the clearest route for now – straight ahead. As you crest a rise, a 100m detour to the left leads to a cup-and-ring-marked boulder.

There is 'rock art' similar to this scattered throughout Northumberland, made by Neolithic and early Bronze Age people between 3500 and 6000 years ago, but its meaning has been lost in the intervening millennia.

On the main route, keep straight on, choosing the middle of three paths ahead. This broad, grassy route descends to a gate at the bottom of the hill. Soon after this, you reach a rough track.

8 Turn left along the track. Follow it round to the left, passing through two gates between the buildings at **Whittondean**. After the second gate, keep straight ahead along a rough lane. Swing right on joining another track from the left, known as **Hillhead Road**. A short way further on pass to the right of **Sharpe's Folly**. This was built to provide work for unemployed stonemasons. At a fork bear left to reach the road.

9 Turn left and walk along the road for 110m. Just before the next turning, go through a kissing-gate on the right. The grassy path eases its way down to a gate at the top of a lane. Keep left as you descend. On reaching a T-junction, turn left. In 150m, cross the car park on your right to reach the footbridge over the **River Coquet**. Cross this and take the alley straight ahead, signposted 'town centre'. Keep straight on until you reach Front Street. Now turn right to return to the Market Cross.

> ⓘ **With just 2000 inhabitants, Northumberland National Park has the lowest population of all the Parks in England and Wales.**

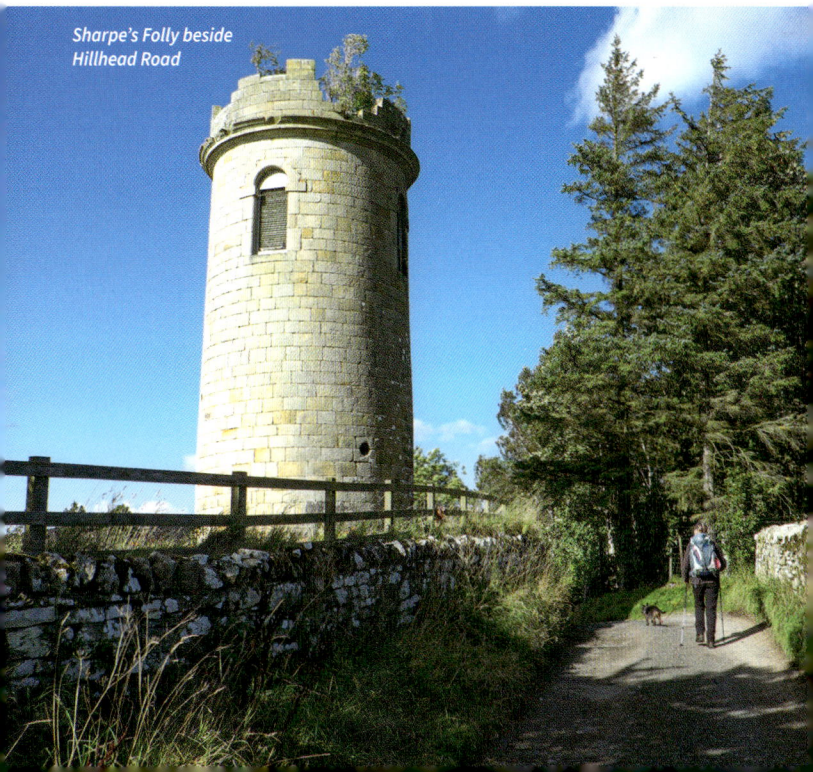

Sharpe's Folly beside Hillhead Road

The moorland above Rothbury

WALK 4
Rothbury Terraces

Start/finish	*Market Cross, Rothbury*
Locate	*NE65 7UT ///dusts.flotation.minus*
Cafes/pubs	*In Rothbury*
Transport	*Buses 16A, 16B, 471 and X14 serve Rothbury*
Parking	*Cowhaugh car park (free) beside River Coquet, Rothbury*
Toilets	*Rothbury town centre*

Time 2hr
Distance 6km (3¾ miles)
Climb 190m

A short, stiff climb leads to gorgeous heather moorland with easy track walking

There's a steep pull from Rothbury on to the low moorland directly above it, but the effort is rewarded many times over. Making use of an old carriage route, this walk winds its gentle way across the open hill, enjoying outstanding views up the Coquet Valley to the Cheviots and across to the Simonside Hills. Visit in late summer, when the heather is in bloom and the moorland is a carpet of vibrant purple.

Rothbury

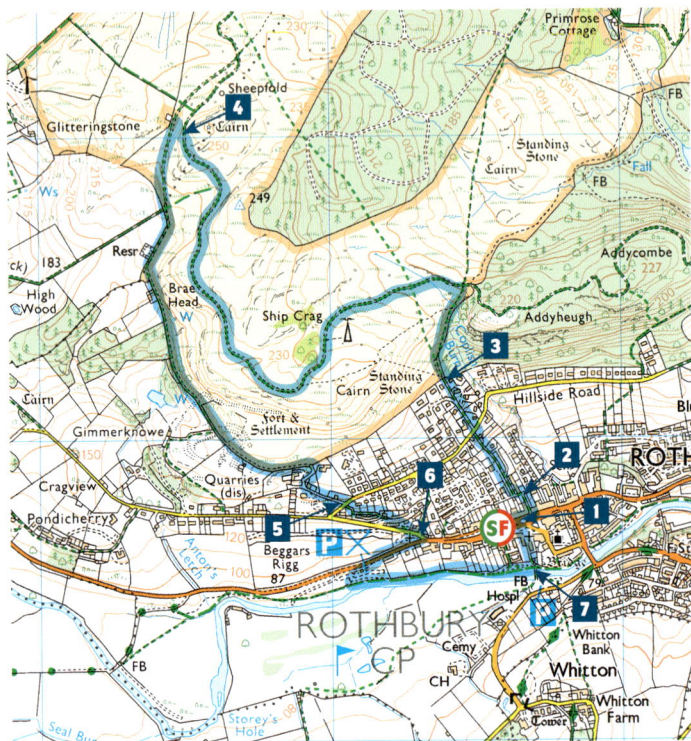

1 Standing on Front Street with your back to the Market Cross, cross the road and climb the steps beside the war memorial. Cross diagonally left to walk up the narrow alley to the left of the Narrow Nick pub, later climbing some steps.

2 Turn left at the top of the steps and then take the lane climbing right. Keep straight on, along the enclosed path to the left of the entrance to Greenacre. At the top of the next set of steps, turn right along the lane and immediately left – up Blaeberry Hill. As the lane starts bending left, take the path to the right of the asphalt. This climbs to a stile on the edge of access land.

3 After crossing the stile, you'll see two paths continuing uphill. Take the less clear, right-hand option, never straying too far from fence on the right as you climb through the light woodland. Emerge from the trees and reach a track. Turn left along this, later passing to the right of the telecoms mast near **Ship Crag**. Follow the track for almost 2km, all the while soaking up the wonderful sense of space on these moors. Having ignored a few narrow trails to the left, you'll arrive at a slightly wider path dropping towards a small group of trees beside a wall.

4 Take this path. On reaching the wall, turn left and follow this clear path as it mirrors part of the outward route but at a lower level. Having followed it for 1km – sometimes on grass, briefly on concrete and latterly on gravel – pass through a gate and drop to a surfaced lane. Turn right along this and follow it down to the left to reach a T-junction.

5 At the junction, cross diagonally right to pick up an enclosed path on the other side of the wall. As this opens out, descend the concrete steps and turn left along a residential road for about 40m. Now take the footpath signposted to the right. At a road, turn left to reach the T-junction with the **B6341**.

In late summer, the flowering heather creates a carpet of purple

The lower, woodland section in autun

6 Turn right along the main road, a pavement materialising after 80m. In a further 90m, take the path signposted left to the riverside path. Cross a parking area diagonally right to continue downhill, now on a surfaced path. This zigzags its way down to a surfaced riverside path, where you turn left. Follow this path for 650m – until you see the footbridge over the River Coquet on your right. Watch for various species of tits, including flocks of excitable long-tailed tits, flitting about among the willows and other trees along the riverbank.

7 Don't cross the footbridge; instead, turn left along an alley, signposted 'town centre'. Keep straight on until you reach Front Street. Now turn right to return to the Market Cross.

Cragside Estate

The moorland track on this walk is just one of the 50km of carriage drives created on the Cragside Estate for Lord Armstrong and his guests to enjoy. A grammar school-educated Newcastle lad and son of a corn merchant, Armstrong made much of his fortune from hydraulic machinery, armaments and naval gunships. In 1887, he was made Baron Armstrong of Cragside, and became the first engineer to enter the House of Lords. A short drive from Rothbury, the house and grounds at Cragside are now owned by the National Trust and are open to the public.

WALK 5
South from Amble

Time 2¼hr
Distance 7.5km
(4¾ miles)
Climb 55m

Gentle walking through dunes and across farmland, with an optional visit to a nature reserve

Start/finish	Amble harbour
Locate	NE65 0AP ///stag.starred.earphones
Cafes/pubs	In Amble and at Hauxley Nature Reserve
Transport	Buses X18 and X20 stop about 700m from start of walk
Parking	Harbourside car parks
Toilets	Near harbour and at Hauxley Nature Reserve

This gentle, lollipop-shaped walk starts from the harbourside town of Amble, at the mouth of the River Coquet, and follows the England Coast Path south through the dunes. Heading inland, you then cross farmland and use quiet lanes to reach Hauxley Nature Reserve before returning to the coast for an easy stroll back to Amble.

The coast south of Amble

1 The walk starts from Coquet House, the Harbour Commissioners' building. With your back to Coquet House and facing out to sea, turn right along the path at the back of the harbour. Turn left to walk beside blue railings. At the far end of the harbourside path, turn right and climb the steps beside a row of houses. Go straight across Cliff House's driveway and enter Paddlers Park.

2 In the park, fork right. You are now following signs for the **England Coast Path** and continue to do so for just under 2.5km. At the far end of the fenced children's play area, turn left. The path bends right. Beyond the red lifebuoy, follow the trail uphill through dune grasses, bearing right at an early fork. Keep to the seaward side of an open area and, after crossing a lane, pass to the left of the **cemetery**.

3 At the far corner of the cemetery wall, the England Coast Path goes sharp right and then left along the edge of another open area. Drop into the **Amble Links** car park, walk towards the sea and then take the path on the right along the top of low cliffs. There are views of Coquet Island and its lighthouse off to your left. Drawing level with the southern end of the holiday park, go straight over a beach access path. Continue on the clearest trail until you reach a junction of routes near a litter bin and gate beside the road.

Looking across the fields to Coquet Island

Looking back to Amble from the coast path

High Hauxley

> ⓘ *The River Coquet rises high in the Cheviot Hills and winds its way for about 90km (56 miles) to enter the North Sea at Amble.*

4 Go through the gate, turn left along the road and then, after just a few metres, enter the field on your right at a fingerpost. Keep to the left-hand edge of this field. When the hedgerow on your left ends, turn left, walking along an uncultivated strip to reach a rough track beside buildings at **High Hauxley**.

5 Turn right along the track and left at the road. When the road bends left, take the surfaced lane on the right. Bear right when this splits, quickly passing through a gate. The next gate leads into **Hauxley Nature Reserve**. While the main route does not enter the reserve, walkers without dogs can opt to visit the site and complete a circuit of its waymarked trail.

6 Just before the gate, take the shady path on the left. Turn left on reaching a shared-use path. This broadens to become a rough vehicle track. Turn right on reaching a surfaced lane in **Low Hauxley**. Go right again at a T-junction and walk along the road for 190m – until you see an England Coast Path sign, just after the last building.

7 Turn right along the coast path. After just 100m, there is a trail on the left dropping into a car park. Ignoring this, continue along the top of the dunes. Keep right at the next waymark post and then, 350m beyond the car park, bear left at a second waymark. This returns to the gate at Waypoint 4.

Don't go through; instead bear right and retrace your outward steps to Amble.

✚ To lengthen

A circuit of the waymarked trail around Hauxley Nature Reserve, starting from Waypoint 6, adds about 45min to the walk.

Hauxley Nature Reserve

The nature reserve at Hauxley, open all year, occupies part of a former open-cast coal mine, having been bought by the Northumberland Wildlife Trust in 1983. The site incorporates a lake and meadows where species include a variety of waterfowl, wildflowers, butterflies and dragonflies. There is a circular walk around the entire site, one wheelchair-accessible trail, six hides, a play area and a cafe. Admission is free but donations are encouraged. No dogs allowed. The site opens at 9am and closes at 5.30pm (5pm in winter).

Bird sculpture at the entrance to Hauxley Nature Reserve

WALK 6
North from Alnmouth

Time 1¾hr
Distance 5km
(3 miles)
Climb 70m

Visit one of Northumberland's finest beaches and walk beside a wildlife-rich estuary

Start/finish	Alnmouth Beach
Locate	NE66 3NJ ///unloading.droplet.breezy
Cafes/pubs	Pubs and cafes in village, Foxton Hall clubhouse at Alnmouth Golf Club
Transport	Buses X18 and X20. Trains to Alnmouth stop outside the village centre, about 1.3km from Waypoint 5
Parking	Alnmouth Beach pay-and-display car park
Toilets	Near clubhouse for Alnmouth Village Golf Course

The village of Alnmouth occupies a pretty spot beside a bay of golden sand, near where the gently winding River Aln briefly widens before entering the sea. This walk starts from that gorgeous beach before climbing gently to join the England Coast Path. After heading inland on quiet lanes, it drops back to the village and follows a riverside path beside saltmarsh and creeks that host a variety of waders and over-wintering waterfowl.

Alnmouth seen from off route

From the old stone lifeboat house at the beachside entrance to the **car park**, follow the surfaced access lane inland. On the far side of the golf course, enter the motorhome parking area on your right. As the route ahead forks, bear left, uphill on a grassy path. Emerging from a section of path enclosed by higher, denser vegetation, you'll see a coastal battery on the right, built in 1861.

> ⓘ *The TV crime drama series 'Vera' was filmed at locations around Northumberland, including Alnmouth, Amble, Bamburgh and Holy Island.*

The golden beach at Alnmouth.

2 Immediately after the battery, the **England Coast Path** joins from the left. Crossing part of a golf course, keep close to the fence on your left. Soon after passing some camping pods, a track is joined. As this bends right, take the path on the left, continuing along the England Coast Path, with views down onto the rocky foreshore. At the next waymarked fork, bear left, heading away from the sea but still following the coast path for now. Make directly for the clubhouse at **Foxton Hall**.

3 Reaching the clubhouse, step onto the patio area and follow it round to the left, always keeping in close to the building on your right. Just after the toilets, turn left along the club's surfaced access lane. Follow it to a T-junction with a minor road, passing several attractive homes along the way, including an interesting art deco-style house.

4 Turn left at the T-junction. As you follow the quiet road descending towards the edge of **Alnmouth**, you're able to look down on a lovely section of the **River Aln**, where it performs several sweeping bends. Entering Alnmouth, turn right at the roundabout – signposted Newcastle and Alnwick – and continue along the **B1338** as far as the bridge over the River Aln.

Among the bird species you might spot beside the River Aln estuary are greenshank, sandpiper, little egret, curlew, lapwing, oyster-catcher, teal and wigeon.

The meandering River Aln

5 Immediately before the bridge, go through the gate on the left to join the signposted England Coast Path. A set of steps drops you onto a riverside path that winds its way along the edge of the estuary. On reaching a lane in Alnmouth, turn right. At a T-junction, go right again – along Marine Road. As this road bends left, turn right as if to enter the car park for Alnmouth Village Golf Club, but then, just before the parking area itself, follow the signposted path to the right. Passing between the beach and the links course, a path leads back to the car park. Don't forget to drop onto the beach – from either this path or the car park – for the opportunity to feel the sand between your toes!

(i) *As well as the National Park, there are two National Landscapes in the county: the North Pennines and the Northumberland Coast.*

– To shorten

At the roundabout just before Waypoint 5, carry straight on. As The Wynd bends left, continue straight ahead along Northumberland Street and through the main part of the village. Reaching the seafront, rejoin the main route by turning left along Marine Road. This cuts about 15min off the walk.

Golfing first

This walk passes two golf clubs. The nine-hole links course in the village is the oldest of its type in England, having been established in 1869 by the Scottish golfer Mungo Park. The 18-hole course at Foxton Hall opened in 1931. Although the two were once part of the same club, the links course is now run by Alnmouth Village Golf Club while the newer course is part of Alnmouth Golf Club.

The links course at Alnmouth

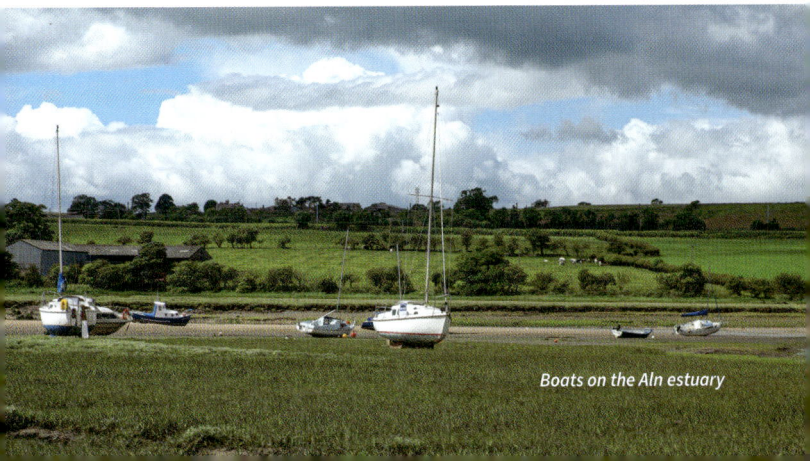

Boats on the Aln estuary

Looking upstream towards Lion Bridge

WALK 7
Alnwick Castle and riverside

Time 1¼hr
Distance 4km
(2½ miles)
Climb 50m

Stroll through an historic town and riverside meadows with castle views

Start/finish	Bondgate Tower, Alnwick
Locate	NE66 1SX ///snores.intersect.bands
Cafes/pubs	Pubs and cafes in town centre
Transport	Buses X15 and X20
Parking	Greenwell Road car park
Toilets	On Greenwell Road

As well as exploring the historic market town of Alnwick – wandering cobbled alleyways and passing through the last remaining section of the town walls – this walk takes in a lovely meadow beside the River Aln. This gentle riverside section is dominated by Alnwick Castle, home to the Duke and Duchess of Northumberland. After your walk, consider visiting the castle or some of the town's other attractions, including the Alnwick Garden.

Bondgate

Alnwick

1 With your back to the Bondgate (Hotspur) Tower and facing away from the town centre, take the road on the left, Greenwell Road. Follow it round to the left and past the car parks. At the end of the road, descend the slope to the right and then swing left along the cobbles of Bow Alley. Emerging on Narrowgate, turn right. As you descend towards the river, you pass one of the gates of **Alnwick Castle** on your right. Use the road bridge, known as **Lion Bridge**, to cross the River Aln. The 'Percy'

lion on the bridge was sculpted by John Knowles in 1773. It features a straight tail, a symbol of the Percy family, which includes the Duke and Duchess of Northumberland.

2 Immediately after the bridge, turn right through the pedestrian gate. With the river on your right, follow the riverside path downstream through a huge meadow. The castle looms on the far side of the water. Beyond the castle, pass a **weir** and then come to a fence.

3 Cross the step stile in the fence and continue along the riverbank – with a lightly wooded embankment to your left. About 130m beyond the stile, in a clearer area, turn sharp left, heading back on yourself on a slightly higher path. Emerging from the trees, keep straight ahead on a faint, grassy trail leading to a gate. The giant 'golf ball' on top of Alnwick Moor in the distance is one of the RAF's remote radar sites, helping to defend UK airspace.

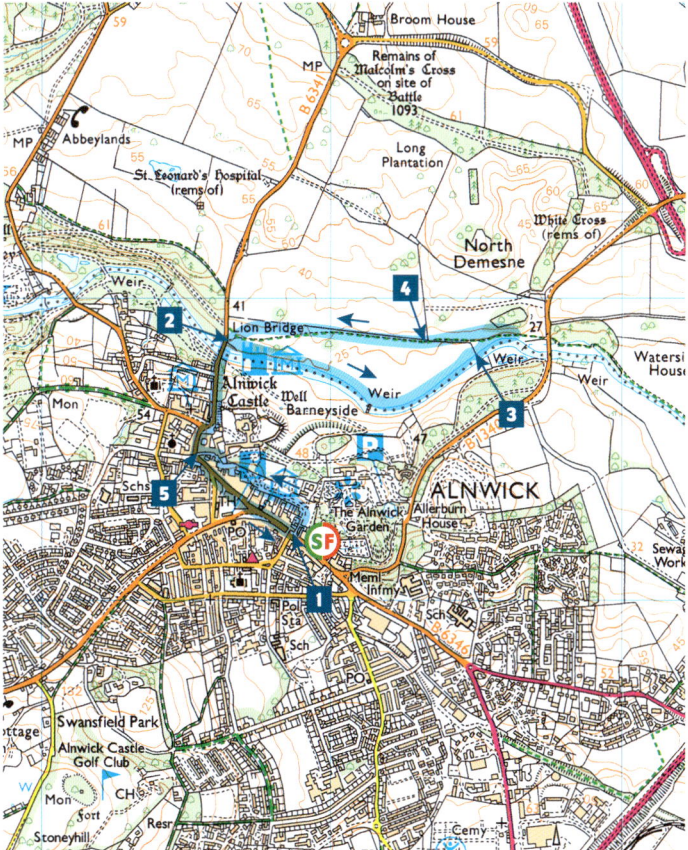

Alnwick Castle looms over the river

4 Go through the gate, re-entering the huge riverside meadow you were in earlier but higher up the slope. Walk with the fence on your right for about 600m. Then, on nearing the far side of the field, swing left to descend back towards the gate on the north side of Lion Bridge at Waypoint 2. (The path is unclear here.) Go through the gate, turn left to cross the bridge and retrace your steps as far as Bow Alley.

5 Instead of turning left along Bow Alley, continue on the pavement, following the road round to the left, still on Narrowgate. Keep left where Fenkle Street goes up to the right. Narrowgate then becomes Bondgate Within. Pass through the pedestrian passageway to the left of Bondgate Tower to return to the start point.

Bondgate Tower, also known as Hotspur Tower, was built in the middle of the 15th century by the second Earl of Northumberland. It forms the east gate of the former town wall. The road through the town centre is known as Bondgate Within; after it passes through the gate, it is called Bondgate Without.

(i) Sir Thomas Percy, an ancestor of the present Duke of Northumberland, was hanged, drawn and quartered for treason in 1537.

+ To lengthen

To explore more of the town, turn right along Bailiffgate as you draw level with the castle gates on your left. Beyond the museum, turn left along Northumberland Street. Go left through the archway in Pottergate Tower and then turn right at the next T-junction to rejoin the route at Waypoint 5. This adds about 10min to the walk.

Alnwick Castle

The massive, 14th-century castle at Alnwick is still lived in by the Percy family, making it the UK's second largest inhabited castle after Windsor. Open to the public, it has become particularly popular with visitors since it was used in the filming of two of the *Harry Potter* films, playing the role of the famous Hogwarts School of Witchcraft and Wizardry.

Alnwick Castle gatehouse

A bench is passed on the descent from Brough Law

WALK 8
Brough Law

Start/finish	*Ingram*
Locate	*NE66 4LT ///tend.crest.stood*
Cafes/pubs	*Cafe in Ingram*
Transport	*No public transport*
Parking	*National Park car park (free) at Ingram Bridge*
Toilets	*Beside Ingram Cafe and at Bulby's Wood car park*

Time 2hr
Distance 6km (3¾ miles)
Climb 190m

A steady climb on grass to an ancient hilltop settlement followed by a steep descent

Brough Law lies on the eastern edge of the Cheviot Hills and provides excellent views into the heart of these remote uplands. The walk up to it passes various prehistoric earthworks and the 300m-high summit is crowned by an Iron Age hill fort, the stone ramparts of which are still clearly visible. The climb has some moderately steep sections and is briefly unclear; the descent is steeper.

Re-entering Ingram at the end of the walk

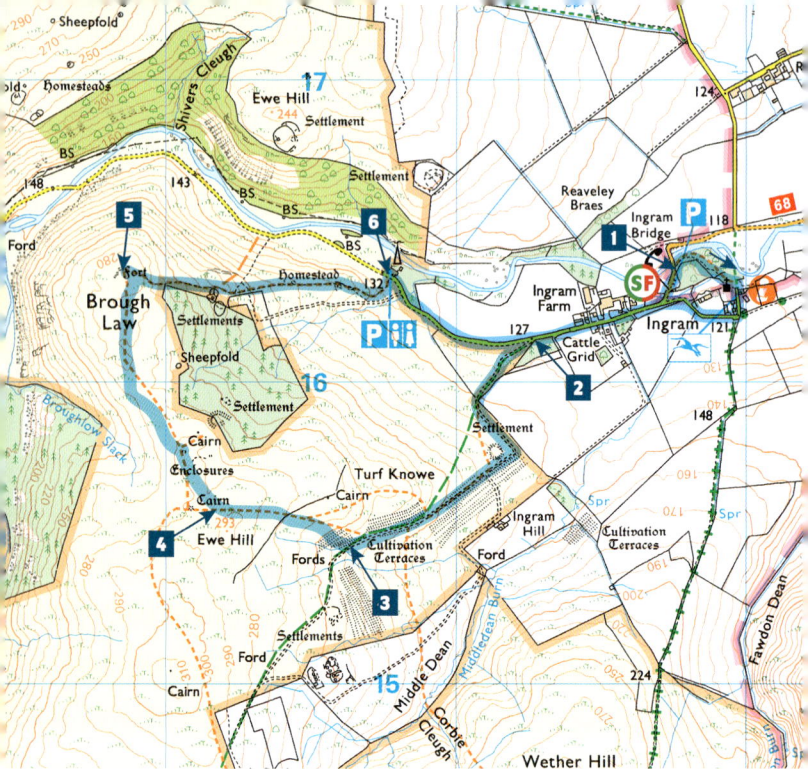

1 Standing in the car park facing the road, take the path to the right – signposted to the church. This emerges in the car park for Ingram Cafe. Immediately turn right along the access lane. Follow this round a sharp bend to the right beyond the **church**. Keep left at the next junction – signposted Linhope, Hartside – and follow this quiet road for 480m, later crossing a cattle grid.

2 About 150m beyond the cattle grid, take the broad, stony track rising left. Follow this round a left bend at a waymark post and then a sharp right bend. A mound to the right here marks the site of an old settlement. When the track bends left, keep straight ahead along a grassy route, ignoring a faint path forking right. You pass one waymark post with an unclear route shown to the right. Ignore this and continue to a second post.

A grassy track makes its way towards Brough Law

> **ⓘ** *The feral goats that live in the Cheviot Hills are thought to be the descendants of animals reared by early Neolithic people.*

Two Bronze Age burial cairns were uncovered on Turf Knowe just above these waymarks. One of the pots unearthed by archaeologists contained the cremated remains of a child who died, possibly from meningitis, 4000 years ago.

3 Bear right at this second post – following the 'Hillfort Trail'. After a steep climb, the gradient eases and the path swings slightly left. It's indistinct here, but there is a waymark post ahead. The path disappears almost entirely as you near the top of **Ewe Hill** – simply maintain your line and, after about 110m, the way ahead becomes clearer again. You'll soon be able to see higher into the Breamish valley, with Cunyan Crags over to the right. Continue to a fork.

On the descent

4 Bear right at this fork and then keep right on joining another broad path from the left. This winds its way up to the remains of the hill fort on **Brough Law**. It splits in three on the way up. Taking the middle option, cross the outer ring of stones and then, almost immediately, turn left to cross the inner ring.

5 Having explored the hilltop settlement and enjoyed the views, exit the inner ring of stones the same way you entered and then, instead of turning right to retrace your steps through the outer ring, keep straight ahead, through a gap in the stones. Follow the grassy path downhill. Keep left on reaching a fenced area of felled forest and stay with the clearest path, passing a bench along the way. Nearing the base of the hill, the path swings left to drop to the road near the **Bulby's Wood car park**.

6 Turn right along the road. After re-entering **Ingram**, keep left as another lane goes right. The car park where the walk started is on the right in 50m.

ⓘ *The highest point in Northumberland is The Cheviot, rising to 815m above sea level.*

The hill forts of Northumberland

Brough Law is one of many dozens of Iron Age hill forts scattered throughout Northumberland. They were built about 2300 years ago by the Votadini, a tribe of Celts who lived in an area of south-east Scotland and north-east England from the Firth of Forth down to the River Tyne. When the Romans arrived, they were at first ruled directly. Then, after Hadrian's Wall was built and the Romans retreated south, this tribe remained allied with the invaders and formed a 'friendly' buffer between the legionaries and the Pictish tribes further north.

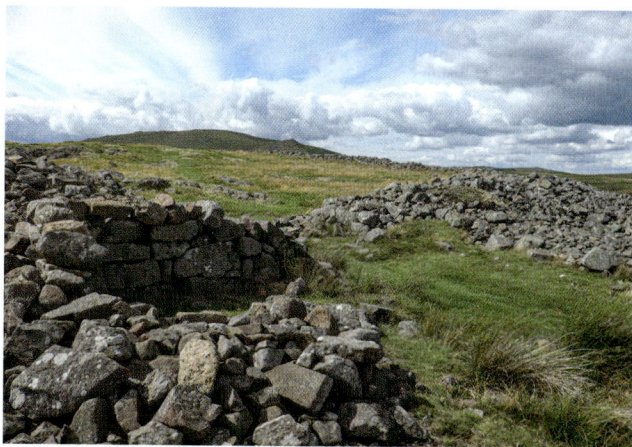

Remains of the hill fort on the summit of Brough Law

Dunstanburgh Castle

WALK 9
Craster and Dunstanburgh Castle

Start/finish	*Craster*
Locate	*NE66 3TW ///seaweed.generally.discrepancy*
Cafes/pubs	*Pubs and cafes in Craster*
Transport	*Buses 418 and X18*
Parking	*Craster Quarry pay-and-display car park*
Toilets	*In car park*

No visit to the Northumberland coast would be complete without a walk to Dunstanburgh Castle. In a county full of impressive castles, this is probably the most striking in terms of location. The route starts with a short exploration of the tiny fishing village of Craster before an easy there-and-back walk to the 14th-century ruins, perched on top of a rocky promontory almost constantly battered by the waves.

Time 1¾hr
Distance 5.5km (3½ miles)
Climb 50m

Amble around a gorgeous fishing village before walking to clifftop castle ruins

The route passes above the pretty harbour

A summer's day at Craster

1 Drop from the top (largest) part of the car park and turn immediately sharp right along a gravel path running behind some houses. This broadens and swings right to reach the top of a surfaced lane. Turn right here, along a gravel track. This later swings left, immediately becoming grass, and then forks.

2 Keep left at the fork. Beyond the edge of **Craster**, go through a kissing-gate and turn left. In a further 30m, bear left at a fork and then go left again along the surfaced coast path.

Keep to the seaward side of the first buildings on the southern edge of the village and to the right of a play area. The coast path then enters the beer garden behind the Jolly Fisherman pub.

ⓘ Howick Hall, near Craster, was the home of the second Earl Grey, the 19th-century British Prime Minister. The bergamot-flavoured Earl Grey tea is named after him.

Stone-built cottages in Craster

3 After a gate on the far side of the beer garden, turn left along a track between the buildings. Go right along the road and follow it down to the left, above the pretty harbour. As you draw level with the small lifeboat station on the left, turn right along a surfaced path. On reaching a cobbled area, turn left and then go right at a T-junction to reach the lane-end.

4 Go through the gate at the lane-end. A second gate gives access to a well-used, grassy path just above the shoreline rocks. After two more gates, keep to the track which then swings up to the left, rougher underfoot now. When the track ends, make directly for **Dunstanburgh Castle** on a grassy path. The

dramatically situated ruins are open to the public, and admission is free to members of English Heritage and the National Trust.

5 Having visited the castle, return to the lane-end gate at Waypoint 4. As the harbourside path you followed earlier goes left, keep straight ahead to reach a T-junction. Turn right – along the pavement – and the Craster Quarry car park is on the left in 200m.

ⓘ *Craster is famous for its kippers and there is still one smokehouse in the village that turns herrings into this smoked breakfast treat.*

— To shorten

Miss out the village loop by leaving the car park via the main entrance and turning right along the road. In 200m, turn left along the lane at the back of the harbour and follow it until it ends – joining the route description at Waypoint 4. This reduces the walk by about 35min.

Dunstanburgh Castle

Occupying a windswept headland of whin sill – the same igneous rock that Hadrian's Wall sits on – Dunstanburgh Castle is one of England's most dramatically located castles. Dating back to 1313, it was built by Earl Thomas of Lancaster, probably as a show of might in his opposition to King Edward II. The only time it saw military action was during the Wars of the Roses in the second half of the 15th century, when it was captured twice by Yorkist forces.

Dunstanburgh Castle's gatehouse

The path winds its way steadily down towards the coast

WALK 10
Newton-by-the-Sea

Time 2¼hr
Distance 7.5km
(4¾ miles)
Climb 60m

A moderate walk across farmland, through dunes and past secluded beaches

Start/finish	High Newton-by-the-Sea
Locate	NE66 3DH ///rail.ferrying.people
Cafes/pubs	Pubs in High Newton and Low Newton
Transport	Bus 418
Parking	High Newton car park (with height barrier)
Toilets	In Low Newton

Newton-by-the-Sea is split in two: the quiet village of High Newton, where this walk starts, and Low Newton, which includes a three-sided square of 19th-century fishermen's cottages beside a small sandy bay. The route crosses farmland with good views of the coast before picking up the England Coast Path. It passes a nature reserve, calls in at Low Newton and then continues through the dunes and past quiet beaches before returning to High Newton.

Looking north into Beadnell Bay

Beadnell Bay

Whittingham Carr

Newton Links

Dunes

Mean High Water

Mean Low Water

7

Snook Point

Link House Farm

St Oswald's Way

Snook

Football Hole

Quarry (dis)

Pern Carr

High Newton-by-the-Sea

High Newton Farm

N C Path

Lobster Ca

Newton Point

Newton Point

Caravan Park

SF

Newton Hall

W

P

1

Quarry (dis)

Quarry House

15

15

St Mary's or Newton Haven

Low Newton-by-the-Sea

Kirk Dike

6

MLW

2

Risemoor Cottage

3

Newton Pool Nature Reserve

Kelsoe Hill

Embleton Links

Fish Carr

Scadpalle

5

MHW

4

Jenny Bells Carr

Dunstanburgh Castle Golf Club

Ford The Skaith

NTL

Embleton Bay

1 Take the path in the corner of the car park opposite the vehicle entrance. On reaching a farm track, turn right. This ends at the entrance to a field 500m from the car park. Don't enter the field – instead, turn right along an indistinct path through long grass with a fence on your right and an intermittent fence on the left for 650m, until the fence on your right ends.

2 Now keep straight ahead, walking with a hedgerow on your left for 50m. Pass to the right of an old wooden fencepost with a yellow waymark on it. The faint trail swings left at the fencepost and then uphill to the right. It keeps to the immediate left of an area of gorse and reaches the highest ground on **Kelsoe Hill**.

3 The trail swings left along the top of this low, grass-covered ridge, with great views of the coast and Dunstanburgh Castle. Cross a narrow, cultivated strip and then continue along the crest of another small ridge. After forking right, the faint trail drops to a broad, grassy path beside a fence.

4 Turn left along this path, soon passing a picnic bench beside a concrete pillbox. About 180m beyond the picnic bench, the fence bends right. Leave the clear path here by keeping straight ahead on a line through the crops. In 200m, another broad, grassy

path materialises – this time with a fence on the left. Keep close to this fence as you briefly skirt the edge of **Embleton Links** golf course to reach a T-junction.

5 Turn left here, along the England Coast Path. Keep to the clearest path at all times, ignoring trails to the right. After 300m, pass a bird hide looking out over the **Newton Pool Nature Reserve**. This rush-fringed pool and wetland area is owned by the National Trust and is a good place to spot herons, waders and waterfowl. Follow the coast path for 500m and reach a surfaced lane that passes between the buildings at **Low Newton-by-the-Sea**. Follow this round to the right to emerge onto a road. The fishermen's cottages and pub are to the right, as is the beach at Newton Haven.

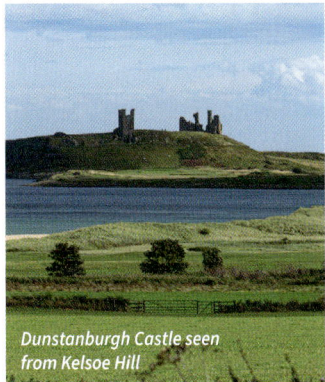

Dunstanburgh Castle seen from Kelsoe Hill

In the dunes above Football Hole

— To shorten

To miss out the farmland section of the walk, turn right out of the car park and follow the road down into Low Newton-by-the-Sea. About 50m short of the fishermen's cottages, go through the gate on the right – Waypoint 6 in the walk description. This reduces the walk by 45min.

6 Turn left along the road for 50m and then go through the gate on the right. Faced with two paths, take the right-hand option. After 900m, the coast path reaches **Newton Point**. The headland has some old Ministry of Defence buildings dating from the Cold War era. The path swings left, later curling around the back of the small, secluded beach at **Football Hole**. Continuing through the dunes, ignore all trails to the left for now. Ahead you'll see the long beaches of Beadnell Bay. The path climbs beside a line of barbed wire to pass through the dunes above the southernmost of these beaches. Watch for an England Coast Path waymark in a further 170m.

7 Fork left at this waymark, dropping to a stile. Cross this to enter the Newton Steads car park. Turn left along the lane and follow it for almost 1km to a T-junction in **High Newton-by-the-Sea**. Turn right and, in a further 70m, take the rough track on the left. A path on the right leads back into the car park in 75m.

WALK 11
St Cuthbert's Way from Wooler

Start/finish	The Black Bull, Wooler
Locate	NE71 6BY ///examples.swimsuits.sheep
Cafes/pubs	Pubs and cafes in Wooler
Transport	Buses 266, 464, 473 and 710
Parking	Padgepool Place car park (free) on Burnhouse Road
Toilets	In short-stay car park next to the Black Bull

The first of two walks from the friendly town of Wooler, this route follows the waymarked St Cuthbert's Way east, climbing steadily via roads and good paths onto Weetwood Moor. After crossing the open moorland, covered in heather, bilberry and gorse, it follows a series of byways around the edge of the high ground, enjoying superb views of the Cheviot Hills.

Time 2¾hr
Distance 8.5km (5¼ miles)
Climb 190m

A steady climb, via the St Cuthbert's Way, onto heather moorland with superb views

On Weetwood Moor

Church Street, Wooler

1 With your back to the Black Bull, turn left along the road and then left down Church Street. After 160m, turn right along a path between the houses and then follow the gravel lane to the A697. Turn left and take the next turning on the right. After crossing **Wooler Water**, turn right again into a small car park and then walk beside the bowling green and children's play area. Keep straight ahead to emerge on another road.

2 Turn left along the road, which later climbs. After 900m, you reach a sharp right bend. Leave the road by taking the signposted **St Cuthbert's Way** to the left of the bend. Hugging a ledge on the hillside, this narrow path provides good views across the surrounding countryside. After a gate, you enter the access land of **Weetwood Moor**. Continue climbing for a further 380m until, on cresting a rise, a waymark post is reached.

> Weetwood Moor is home to variety of birds. Watch for skylark, golden plover and stonechat on the moorland, and listen for yellowhammers as you walk the byways later. The yellowhammer's song sounds like the bird is calling 'a-little-bit-of-bread-and-no-cheese'.

3 Leaving the St Cuthbert's Way, head right at this post and immediately left along a bridleway. Keep left

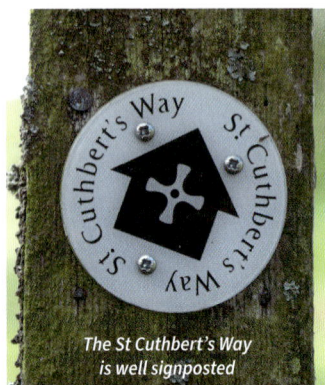

The St Cuthbert's Way is well signposted

at a faint fork 300m beyond the post. A crossing of ways follows in a further 65m. Turn left here and, in just 80m, turn right to rejoin the route of the waymarked bridleway. Keep left at

another faint fork in 300m, following the bridleway to a gate in a fence on the edge of the access land.

4 Go through the gate and follow the trail through tall grasses to a lane. Turn right. When the lane swings left through a gate, keep straight ahead, now on a rough track past **Whitsunbank Hill**. A gate on the right later provides access to the trig pillar if you want – otherwise, keep straight on along the byway. There are superb views ahead to the highest of the Cheviot Hills, including Hedgehope Hill and The Cheviot. The track bends left, through a gate. Just 35m after bending right – where a track joins from the left – reach a track junction.

The route leaves the access land via a gate

Trig pillar on Whitsunbank Hill

5 Turn sharp right at this junction. After just over 1km you join a surfaced lane near a radio mast. Follow this steeply downhill. After 400m, the lane bends left, rejoining the outward route. Now retrace your steps to **Wooler**.

ⓘ *Wooler Hostel was built in World War 2 for members of the Women's Land Army, who did the work of male farm labourers conscripted into the armed forces.*

St Cuthbert's Way

The St Cuthbert's Way is a 100km trail linking Melrose in the Scottish Borders with Lindisfarne in Northumberland. These are the two monasteries most closely associated with St Cuthbert, a 7th-century bishop and hermit renowned for his piety. The waymarked route climbs the Eildon Hills above Melrose and skirts the northern edge of the Cheviot Hills. From Wooler, it heads towards the coast, passing St Cuthbert's Cave, where the monks of Lindisfarne brought their former bishop's body when their island was threatened by Viking raiders. It ends by crossing the sands to the holy island of Lindisfarne.

Leaving the forest via a small gate

WALK 12
Wooler Common

Time 2½hr
Distance 6.5km (4 miles)
Climb 220m

A steep climb to forest and common land on the edge of the Cheviot Hills

Start/finish	The Black Bull, Wooler
Locate	NE71 6BY ///examples.swimsuits.sheep
Cafes/pubs	Pubs and cafes in Wooler
Transport	Buses 266, 464, 473 and 710
Parking	Padgepool Place car park (free) on Burnhouse Road
Toilets	In short-stay car park next to the Black Bull

The second walk in this book from Wooler explores the woods and commons to the west of the town, again using the waymarked St Cuthbert's Way for the first few kilometres. Sitting on the edge of the Cheviot Hills, this area has a remote feel to it and yet is relatively easy to reach. A picnic area about halfway through the walk provides a great spot to rest and enjoy the wildlife around you.

Wooler town centre

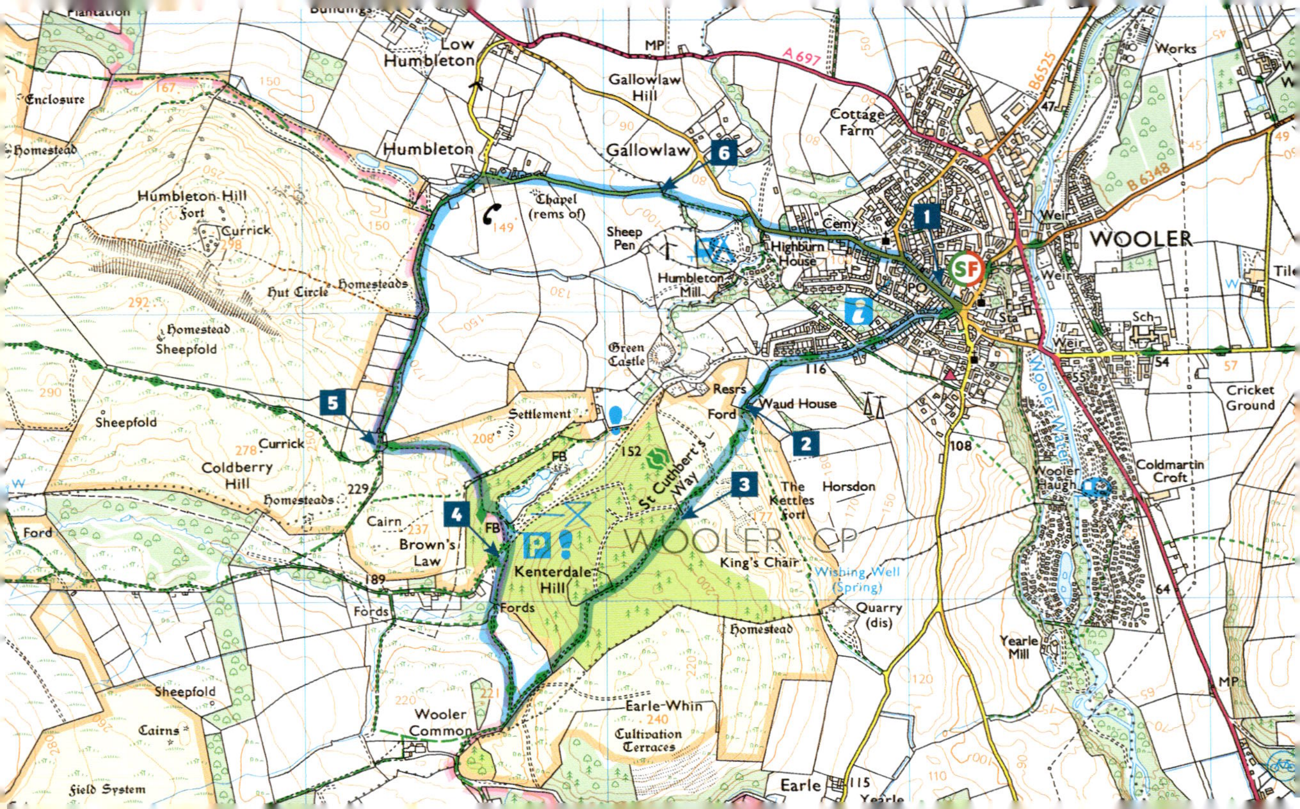

WOOLER
Wooler Water
Low Humbleton
Humbleton
Gallowlaw Hill
Gallowlaw
Cottage Farm
Humbleton Hill
Fort
Currick
Hut Circle
Homesteads
Homestead
Sheepfold
Enclosure
Chapel (rems of)
Sheep Pen
Highburn House
Humbleton Mill
Cemy
PO
Sta
Sch
Weir
Green Castle
Resrs
Ford
Waud House
The Kettles
Fort
Horsdon
Settlement
FB
St Cuthbert's Way
WOOLER CP
King's Chair
Wishing Well (Spring)
Quarry (dis)
Kenterdale Hill
Fords
Cairn
Brown's Law
Coldberry Hill
Currick
Wooler Common
Earle Whin
Cultivation Terraces
Earle
Yearle Mill
Wooler Haugh
Coldmartin Croft
Cricket Ground
Works
Field System
Cairns
A697
B6525
B6348
MP
1
2
3
4
5
6

1 With your back to the Black Bull, turn left along the road. After 70m, turn right up Ramsey's Lane. For the next 3.5km, the route follows the waymarked **St Cuthbert's Way**. About 650m after joining Ramsey's Lane, which becomes Common Road, take the rough track rising left. (This is 200m beyond the last house on the left-hand side of the road.) The track becomes a path between fences and hedgerows, ending at a small gate.

2 Go through the gate and immediately bear right. At a fork next to old wooden fenceposts, bear left. When the path starts climbing, keep to the clearest route. Go straight over a crossing of ways, aiming for the conifer plantation ahead, part of Forestry England's Wooler Common. Just a few metres back from a gate leading into the forest, bear left at a fork, soon entering the forest via a higher gate.

3 Beyond this gate, a trail heads uphill through a felled area. Keep left as you cross the highest ground on **Kenterdale Hill**, soon descending on a clear path through trees. Leave the forest via a small gate and continue with a fence on your left for 150m. On reaching a waymark post, turn sharp right – almost back on yourself. Go through a gate and follow the trail to a minor road.

4 Turn right along the road and immediately left into a **car park** beside a picnic area. Cross a small bridge to the left of the information boards and then, in a further 50m, take the waymarked path climbing left through the trees. After leaving the woods via a gate, keep straight ahead on a grassy path climbing gently to another gate.

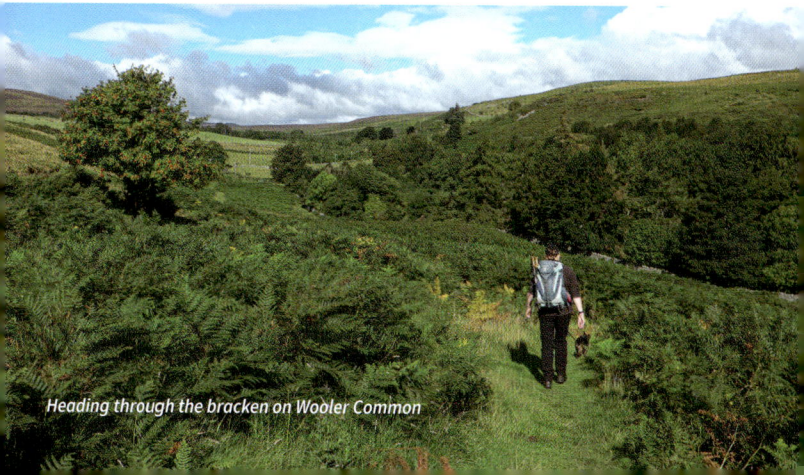

Heading through the bracken on Wooler Common

Humbleton

The woods around the picnic area are home to a range of trees including larch, sycamore, sitka spruce, Scots pine and Corsican pine. Alder, which loves wet ground, can be seen beside the ponds.

5 Go through this gate and, leaving the St Cuthbert's Way, bear right and right again. You soon head downhill on a track. After passing beneath **Humbleton Hill**, this becomes a surfaced lane. Take the next lane on the right and follow this downhill through **Humbleton**. After 650m you will see a path on the right, by a bench.

6 Take this path along the field edge and then through a gate. The way ahead is briefly unclear now. Keep straight ahead, ignoring a track swinging right towards a campsite entrance, and drop to a gate beside the road.

Turn right along the road. Turn right again at a T-junction to walk along the main road through **Wooler**. The Black Bull is on the left in about 200m.

− To shorten
From Waypoint 4, instead of turning left into the car park, continue down the road to the T-junction with the main road through Wooler. Turn left to return to the Black Bull. This cuts the walk by 35min.

+ To lengthen
Having followed the track downhill from Waypoint 5 for 450m, go through the gate in the wall on your left and climb the steep path to explore the remains of the fort on Humbleton Hill. Return to the gate and turn left to rejoin the main route. This adds 35min to the route.

WALK 13
Bamburgh

Time 2hr
Distance 7km
(4¼ miles)
Climb 90m

Gentle coastal walking with far-reaching views and lots of historical interest

Start/finish	Bowling Green, Bamburgh
Locate	NE69 7BJ ///shed.iteration.targeted
Cafes/pubs	Pubs and cafes in Bamburgh
Transport	Buses X18 and 418
Parking	Links Road long-stay car park (pay-and-display)
Toilets	Church Street, Bamburgh

After passing beneath the imposing walls of Bamburgh Castle, this walk heads out along the England Coast Path. As it rounds Budle Point, walkers are treated to breathtaking views across the bay and the immense Ross Back Sands towards Holy Island. The return route climbs slightly before heading along quiet lanes and through farmland back to historic Bamburgh, home of the RNLI Grace Darling Museum.

Blackrocks Point and lighthouse

1 Standing beside the **B1340** with your back to **Bamburgh Castle**, take the surfaced path beside the bowling green – passing directly below the castle walls. Beyond the castle, keep straight on, descending to a T-junction in the dunes. Turn left along the **England Coast Path** and keep left at two forks in the dunes. Turn right along a rough track, soon reaching a road.

> ⓘ *Dozens of pillboxes were built along Northumberland's coast in the early years of World War 2 when there was a threat of seaborne Nazi invasion.*

Like Dunstanburgh, Bamburgh Castle sits on a whin sill outcrop. Parts of the building are Norman, but it was restored by the Tyneside industrialist William Armstrong after he bought it at the end of the 19th century.

2 Turn right along the road, with the lighthouse at **Blackrocks Point** ahead. After 1km, the road ends at **Bamburgh Castle Golf Course**. Following the St Oswald's Way for the next 2km, head through the gate onto the golf course. A series of blue-topped posts leads the way. You cross one fairway early on and, after that, walk mostly on the seaward side of the course. Later, you're able to look straight across Budle Bay to the long beach at Ross Back Sands, leading almost all the way to Holy Island. Just over 1km after first stepping onto the golf course – as you pass around the back of a concrete pillbox – there's a waymark post.

3 Take the path heading steeply up the embankment on the left here. At the top, blue posts lead across the western edge of the golf course. After a kissing-gate, drop to a lane and turn left along it for 70m. Go through the large gate set back on the left. A broad, grassy path passes to the right of the buildings at **Newtown** to reach a T-junction of routes.

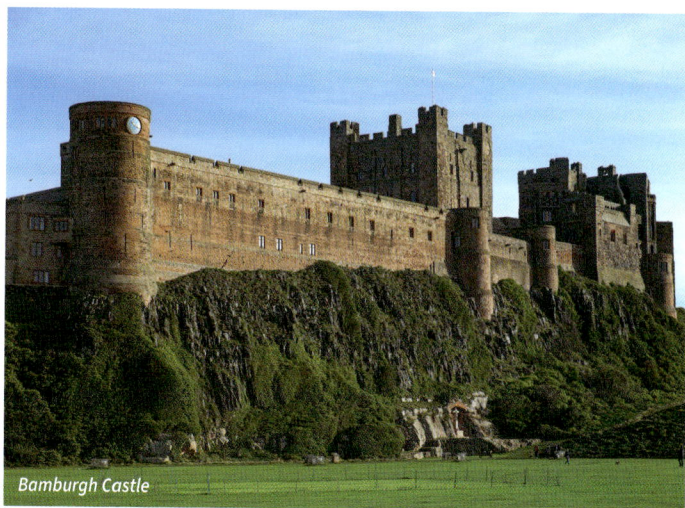

Bamburgh Castle

Looking back across Budle Bay

Ross Back Sands

4 Cross the track here, head to the fence on the left and follow it up the side of the field. Beyond the next kissing-gate, you're back on the golf course. Bear slightly right to follow the now familiar, blue-topped posts to a gate. Go through and turn left along the grass verge beside the **B1342** for 100m.

5 Take the next lane on the right, signposted Dukesfield. Just before the last buildings at the lane-end, cross the stile on the left. Walk beside the fence on the right. On the far side of this field, the grassy trail comes away from the fence slightly to cross

another stile. A trail leads through long grass to cross a third stile. Walk along the right-hand edge of the field to one final stile providing access to the **B1341**.

6 Turn left along the road, joining a roadside path after 240m. After re-entering **Bamburgh**, take the first through road on the left, opposite the Victoria Hotel. At the T-junction, the main route goes right. The Grace Darling Museum is 80m to the left and the churchyard containing her grave is opposite the junction. Drop towards the castle to return to the starting point.

> ⓘ *The Farne Islands, visible off the coast of Northumberland, are renowned for their wildlife, including grey seals, puffins and terns.*

▬ To shorten

Having joined the B1342, ignore the turning at Waypoint 5 and simply follow the road back into Bamburgh, cutting the walk by about 20min.

The courage of Grace Darling

Grace Darling was born in Bamburgh, the daughter of a lighthouse keeper based on the Farne Islands. She became a national heroine when, in September 1838, she risked her life to help save nine people from the steamship *Forfarshire* after it had run aground in a storm. The story of her bravery made international news. The RNLI Museum in Bamburgh tells the story of the rescue and of Grace's life. The memorial to her in St Aidan's churchyard opposite the museum was designed by the renowned 19th-century architect Anthony Salvin.

Grace Darling's grave

WALK 14
Holy Island (Lindisfarne)

Time 1¾hr
Distance 6km
(3¾ miles)
Climb 25m

Enjoy an easy walk around this fascinating tidal island rich with wildlife and historic interest

Start/finish	Holy Island (Lindisfarne)
Locate	TD15 2SE ///rational.grunt.nitrogen
Cafes/pubs	Cafes and pubs on Holy Island
Transport	Bus 477
Parking	Chare End car park on Holy Island (pay-and-display)
Toilets	In village

With a castle and one of Britain's most important ecclesiastical ruins, Holy Island has a special feel to it – possibly partly due to it being cut off from the mainland twice a day. While most tourists focus on the area around the village, this walk explores the quieter, wildlife-rich dunes at the northern end of the island before visiting the more popular attractions. Consult tide timetables before crossing the causeway to the island.

Willow sculpture of a lapwing

Lindisfarne Castle was rebuilt in the early part of the 20th century

1 From the car park entrance, turn right along the road for 230m. Just before dropping to the causeway, take the **England Coast Path** signposted through a gate on the right. In 500m, bear right at a clear fork – this is immediately after an unusual, partially stone-lined feature to the right of the path. In another 250m, bear right at the next fork, walking with the fence on your right. A path joins from the left after 480m and you quickly reach a gate.

Lindisfarne National Nature Reserve covers a massive 3500 hectares. Rare orchids and butterflies thrive in the dunes, while, in the autumn, huge flocks of brent geese fly in from Svalbard to spend the winter on the saltmarsh and mudflats.

2 Turn left before the gate and, almost immediately, fork left. The waymarked England Coast Path winds its way through the dunes, later joining another trail from the right and then forking right. After the trail bends left, it climbs a short rise to reach a T-junction. Turn right here, soon passing through a small gate.

3 After the gate, follow the raised path, known as The Waggonway, along the eastern side of the island. It passes the bird hide beside **The Lough** and provides views of Bamburgh Castle straight ahead. Soon after going through a gap in a wall, The Waggonway swings right, making for some lime kilns beside **Lindisfarne Castle**. Almost 200m beyond the wall gap, reach a tiny footbridge.

Originally a 16th-century fort, Lindisfarne Castle was rebuilt and refurbished in the Arts and Crafts style by architect Edwin Lutyens between 1903 and 1906. It is now owned by the National Trust and is open to the public.

(i) *The Lindisfarne Gospels, now housed in London's British Library, is a masterpiece of early medieval art created by the Holy Island monks in the 8th century.*

Back Skerrs

Coves Haven

Snipe Point

Castlehead Rocks

Nessend

Keel Head

Caves

The Links

Dunes

Sandham

Emmanuel Head

Holy Island
Lindisfarne

2

3

13

Red Brae

King Charles III England Coastal Path

9

Fords

7

Fords

The Lough

Brides Hole

Chare Ends

Pp Ho

Lough Head

9

Sheldrake Pool

ND CP

St Oswald's Way

St Cuthbert's Way

Path

1

P

SF

St Coombs Farm

The Bungalow

13

Broad Stones

Water Tower

Sch

PO

Bridge Well

Lilburn's Cottage

Bible Law

Scar Jockey

The Basin

P

i

Holy Island

Water

HC

Pepple Well

The Ouse

Riding Stone

Lindisfarne Castle

FB

4

WINERY

Rems of Priory (Benedictine)

5

Steel End

Cockle Stone

Castle Point

Chapel (rems of)

CP Bdy

The Harbour

Hole Mouth

Long Ridge

Ridge End

One of the herring-boat sheds

4 Just before the bridge, bear right to drop to a surfaced path. Turn right along this. After passing directly below the castle's northern ramparts, bear right along its access lane for 600m. Beyond the small bay known as **The Ouse**, turn left along a broad track, reaching a fork after 180m. The track is lined by redundant herring boats that have been flipped over and turned into sheds.

5 Bear right at this fork and, in another 100m, locate a path rising (right) between two of the sheds. Nearing the top of the rise, fork right through the turnstiles. This path passes to the right of the priory ruins

The dunes path is fringed with wildflowers

WALK 14 – HOLY ISLAND (LINDISFARNE)

to emerge at the Crown & Anchor pub. Turn left and, beyond the pub, keep straight ahead to reach a crossing of lanes in front of St Aidan's Winery. Turn right here, signposted St Aidan's RC Church. Go diagonally right at the next crossroads. The car park is on the right in 450m.

> ⓘ *The St Oswald's Way, a 156km walking route from Holy Island to Hadrian's Wall, links sites associated with Oswald, a 7th-century king of Northumbria.*

Lindisfarne, a holy island

A modern statue of St Aidan, the first bishop of Lindisfarne, graces the site of the priory, but the island is more closely associated with St Cuthbert. Briefly Bishop of Lindisfarne from AD685, he died in AD687. His body, said to be undecayed 11 years after his death, caused the island to become a place of pilgrimage and strengthened its reputation as a place of Christian learning. The religious site was abandoned after a Viking raid in AD793. The ruins that exist today are the remains of a priory founded by monks from Durham Cathedral in the 12th century. Entry is free to English Heritage members.

The ruins of the 12th-century priory

An opportunity to rest and look out across the River Tweed

WALK 15
Berwick-upon-Tweed

Time 1½hr
Distance 5km
(3 miles)
Climb 80m

A short walk along the defensive walls of this border town, also taking in cliffs and the River Tweed

Start/finish	*Berwick-upon-Tweed railway station*
Locate	*TD15 1NF ///panic.royal.vows*
Cafes/pubs	*Cafes and pubs in Berwick-upon-Tweed*
Transport	*East Coast Main Line railway. Buses X18, 60, 67, 235, 253, 267, 464 and 477*
Parking	*Castlegate long-stay car park (free)*
Toilets	*In Castlegate short-stay car park*

For such a short walk, this one is surprisingly varied. Starting from the railway station, it samples a section of the town's ramparts, before heading out onto low cliffs and then turning inland. After walking along the top of another section of the substantial Elizabethan walls, you follow the River Tweed upstream, later dropping to river level on a good path. A short climb then leads past the castle ruins and back to the railway station.

Fisherman's Haven

1 With your back to the station building's main entrance, take the access road straight ahead, quickly passing a postbox on your right. Follow the road round to the left to reach a mini-roundabout at the junction with the main road – the **A1167**. Turn right and after 400m pass through a gateway in the town walls.

2 Climb the steps on the left immediately after the gateway and then take the next set of steps on the left to reach the top of the ramparts. Turn right along the surfaced path. Go right again at the next path junction then keep right at two forks to drop to a gate.

3 Go through the gate and turn left, passing through an archway in the town walls, known as Cow Port. Cattle would have been taken through this gateway every morning to reach their grazing pastures and then brought back through at night. About 80m after the lane bends left,

> *The county flower of Northumberland is the bloody crane's-bill, sometimes known as the bloody geranium. It is found in sand dunes and on grassland.*

take the surfaced path on the right, walking with a wall on your right at first. After 340m, you come to some low cliffs near the small bay known as **Fisherman's Haven**.

4 Turn right along a grassy path along the cliffs, keeping to the landward side of a wooden fence. Nearing the far side of the **Magdalene Fields** golf course, ignore a trail dropping left – instead, keep straight ahead to pass below a small car park. Follow the lane to a T-junction near the mouth of the **River Tweed**.

The Pier Maltings and other 19th-century buildings

On top of the town walls

The River Tweed is Europe's largest salmon rod fishery south of the Arctic Circle. Almost 160km long, it rises in Scotland's Lowther Hills, close to the source of the River Clyde, and enters the North Sea at Berwick.

5 Turn right along the lane, soon passing the 19th-century Pier Maltings, originally used to process whale oil. Immediately after going through an archway, turn left to join the walkway along the top of the town walls, still with the river on your left. Passing the cannon at **Fisher's Fort** along the way, follow the wall path for 700m, until you reach the road at Bridge End. The bridge across the river here was built in the early 17th century.

6 Cross the road and walk along the cobbled lane opposite. After this bends right, turn left, keeping to the lower path beside the river. This passes under the 'new' road bridge – dating from the 1920s – and later the railway viaduct, and then through an arch in Berwick Castle's White Wall, which you can see heading steeply up the embankment on the right.

7 Take the next path rising on the right 140m beyond the White Wall. You'll see the remains of Berwick's medieval castle on the right here. After a gate, follow the path up to the left through Coronation Park to reach the road. Turn right and immediately right again along the **A1167**. After 150m, you'll reach the mini-roundabout you passed near the start of the walk. Turn right to retrace your steps to the railway station.

Berwick and border history

Now England's northernmost town, Berwick-upon-Tweed has changed hands between the English and the Scots at least 13 times. The castle seen soon after Waypoint 7 was built in the early 12th century by the Scots and was strengthened by England's King Edward I in 1296. A defensive wall was first built around the town in the 14th century, but the ramparts that exist today date from Elizabethan times. Designed by an Italian military engineer and the only wall of its type in Britain, it features projecting stone bastions that served as gun platforms.

An East Coast Main Line train crossing the viaduct

USEFUL INFORMATION

Tourism organisations

Visit Northumberland www.visitnorthumberland.com

Northumberland National Park www.northumberlandnationalpark.org.uk

Northumberland Coast National Landscape www.northumberlandcoast-nl.org.uk

National Trust www.nationaltrust.org.uk

Tourist information centres

Wooler, The Cheviot Centre, Padgepool Place, tel 01668 282123, email wooler.tic@northumberland.gov.uk

Craster, Craster car park, tel 01665 576007, email craster.tic@northumberland.gov.uk

Berwick-upon-Tweed, Walkergate (upstairs in the library), tel 01670 622155, email berwick.tic@northumberland.gov.uk

Alnwick, Bondgate Without (within Alnwick Playhouse), tel 01670 622152, email alnwick.TIC@northumberland.gov.uk

Accommodation booking

Visit Northumberland has accommodation booking pages at

www.visitnorthumberland.com

Buses

Some of the most useful buses for walks in this guide are:

X18 from Newcastle upon Tyne to Berwick-upon-Tweed

X20 from Newcastle upon Tyne to Alnwick

418 from Alnwick to Belford via the coast

477 from Berwick-upon-Tweed across the causeway to Holy Island (dependent on tide times)

Walking advice and information

Weather forecasts www.metoffice.gov.uk

Safety advice for walking on the hills www.adventuresmart.uk

Attractions

St Mary's Lighthouse https://my.northtyneside.gov.uk/category/635/st-marys-lighthouse

Northumberlandia www.northumberlandia.com

Cragside www.nationaltrust.org.uk/visit and search for Cragside

Alnwick Castle www.alnwickcastle.com

The Alnwick Garden www.alnwickgarden.com

Hauxley Nature Reserve and Discovery Centre www.nwt.org.uk

Dunstanburgh Castle www.english-heritage.org.uk/visit and search for Dunstanburgh Castle

Ad Gefrin (whisky distillery and Anglo-Saxon museum) www.adgefrin.co.uk

Bamburgh Castle www.bamburghcastle.com

RNLI Grace Darling Museum www.rnli.org/find-my-nearest/museums and search for Bamburgh

Lindisfarne Castle www.nationaltrust.org.uk/visit and search for Lindisfarne Castle

Lindisfarne Priory www.english-heritage.org.uk/visit/places and search for Lindisfarne Priory

Berwick-upon-Tweed Barracks www.english-heritage.org.uk/visit/places and search for Berwick-upon-Tweed Barracks

© Vivienne Crow 2024
First edition 2024
ISBN: 978 1 78631 201 3

MIX
Paper | Supporting responsible forestry
FSC® C004791

Printed in Singapore by KHL Printing using responsibly sourced paper.
A catalogue record for this book is available from the British Library.

© Crown copyright 2024 OS PU100012932
All photographs are by the author unless otherwise stated.

CICERONE

Cicerone Press, Juniper House, Murley Moss, Oxenholme Road,
Kendal, Cumbria, LA9 7RL

www.cicerone.co.uk

Updates to this Guide

While every effort is made to ensure the accuracy of guidebooks as they go to print, changes can occur during the lifetime of an edition. Any updates that we know of for this guide will be on the Cicerone website (www.cicerone.co.uk/1201/updates), so please check before planning your trip. We also advise that you check information about transport, accommodation and shops locally. We are always grateful for updates, sent by email to updates@cicerone.co.uk or by post to Cicerone, Juniper House, Murley Moss, Oxenholme Road, Kendal, LA9 7RL.

Register your book: To sign up to receive free updates, special offers and GPX files where available, register your book at www.cicerone.co.uk.